THINK
DIGITAL SUCCESS
Skills & Habits

Edward Spade

Edward Spade

ISBN: 1981410074
ISBN-13: 978-1981410071

DEDICATION

To my parents, John and Nora, who have always been there to help and encourage me to do what is right no matter how good or bad the circumstances may have been. They are truly worth my honor.

I Love You Both!

To my lovely wife, Cassie, who is one of the kindest and most caring people I have ever met. She has continued to love me at times when my behavior and words have been unforgivable.

I Love You!

To my Great children:

Eddie ~ Olivia ~ & Timothy

Each of you will always have a special place in my heart and mind.

I Love You All!

CONTENTS

Edward Spade

1. BUSINESS DEVELOPMENT

Let's start by talking about business development and why it's important to develop your business, and more specifically, the things you need to be focusing on in order to successfully build your business.

Do a Few Things Really Well

The first thing you need to realize is when it comes to success in online business, or really any business for that matter, there are just a few things you need to do well. In some cases, you could even get away with just doing one thing really well.

This is a problem for a lot of new entrepreneurs, a lot of people in general who want to break into business, and they believe they have to be all things to all people.

When you start breaking it down, you start looking at the most successful entrepreneurs, the most successful companies, they were built upon the idea of specialization and the idea of becoming really, really good at providing one thing really, really well.

And so you have to begin to ask yourself as an online entrepreneur, "What is it that makes me unique? What are the skills and practices that I bring to the table that people are going to pay me for? What do I do better than most other people, and what's a craft or what's a skill that I can hone and get even better at so I can get paid even more as I go along?"

It's very important that you have this discussion with yourself early and often, because it's very easy, as business grows and as things get busier and as your schedule becomes more and more hectic, for you to divert your attention in a million different directions.

The thing here is to remind you, focus on doing a few things well or even just one thing well. Maybe you're a great presenter or speaker. Maybe you're great at programming. Maybe you have a knack for doing negotiations and putting teams together or brokering deals between two different companies.

It's really up to you to figure out what that special skill is that you bring to the table and then just work

on doing it really, really well and improving it all the time.

How to Get Even Better

That brings us to our second point here, which is how do you get even better at what you're already good at?

When you focus on the things you do naturally well, the things you want to be paid for in your business, now you're creating the level of specialization that people want to pay you for, and then you begin to ask this question, "How do I get even better at what I'm already good at?"

What you're really saying when you ask this question is, "How do I increase my capacity to get paid even more for the skill that I'm already naturally good at and that I'm already broadcasting myself as an expert in and people are already coming to me for help?"

Maybe you're already getting paid good money to do whatever it is. How do you take it even further? How do you expand that skill and become even better at it, and in turn increasing the amount of revenue you can generate through this skill?

It may seem counterintuitive that as you go deeper into one thing you might think there will be less and less for you to do, but actually it's the opposite.

The more you focus on one particular skill, the more opportunity you see to grow and expand inside that skill.

Again, going back to my example of presenting and speaking, once you get really, really good at one form of speaking, maybe you're a platform speaker and you're hired to speak at conferences, well now you've perfected the art of speaking.

You know how to connect with your audience. You know you can keep people's attention and maybe even motivate them to action.

Now you have all kinds of opportunities to take this to the webinar world or the online presentation world or to become a presentation coach and teach other presenters how to do what you do.

As you get better at what you're already good at, you'll increase your capacity to make more money.

Separate Business and Emotion

Here's another really important thing about business development, and it's the ability for you to separate business and emotion. This is where a lot of entrepreneurs, especially newbie entrepreneurs, fall flat.

Money gets involved and a lot of emotion can get involved with money gets involved into the equation.

It's very important for you to look at every situation. Maybe you're dealing with a customer who is just treating you disrespectfully. Maybe you're dealing with a partner or a former partner. Maybe you're working with outsources to provide you with some content or some kind of material for your business, and they become an abrasive personality or they're the kind of personality you just don't get along with well naturally.

It's very easy to become wrapped up emotionally, whether you feel like you've been ripped off for something you paid for or whether you think you've been slighted by them in a respect fashion, you don't feel like they're respecting you.

Base everything on making a decision that's effective for the business. Your job is to make sure your business stays alive. Separating your emotion from the business is very easy to do, when you look at your business in this way.

If it comes time to let somebody go because they're not a good fit, you can strictly focus on, "This is a business decision, and my business is going to die if I don't make this decision."

It's very easy to remove your emotion from it when you separate yourself from the business. Your job is to keep the business alive, and the more you let emotions come into the equation the less effective you will be at making those often difficult decisions that will keep your business afloat.

Be a Lifelong Student

The best business people are lifelong students. If you look at any successful entrepreneur, even the most celebrated people in the world right now that you might be reading biographies about, take a look at their daily routine and they are always learning.

They're always studying. They're always pushing themselves.

Often, the most successful people you can read about are the most driven. These are the people getting up at 3:00 and 4:00 in the morning and working all hours of the day, and I'm not suggesting you have to work nonstop to be successful, but they're addicted to the growth. They're addicted to becoming students of their craft and becoming better at what they already do well.

They never, ever allow themselves to rest on their laurels or look at things they've done in the past and say, "I've already achieved my maximum level of success. I'm done now."

They're always looking to expand. They're students, and when they feel they've mastered something, they go into another area that can expand what they're already doing well and they become a brand new student in that area.

They enjoy the process of learning. They enjoy the process of breaking down something they don't know how to do yet, going through the initial awkward phases of figuring out how this whole thing works, building up proficiency and then they thrive on the idea of mastering something new that they haven't been able to do before.

You need to be able to think that way in all areas of your business.

If there's something you've mastered and it's time to move on, what is another area of your business that you can now master that will make you more profitable?

Repeatable Processes and Systems

Next, you need to be able to find repeatable processes and systems. It's very easy to think of one project you want to launch and that makes you some money, then you put it away and go onto something else and each and every time you're inventing the process. You're starting from scratch.

You need to begin to ask yourself, "How can I leverage the actions I'm taking, the things I'm doing in each project, each revenue-generating project? How can I template these things? How can I write a system or a checklist so that I can repeat a lot of the things that created success in the first place?"

As an example, let's say you create a product of some sort and people are buying your work and you get questions. Maybe the questions come in and a lot of them are the same type of question. Maybe they fall into three different categories, but for the most part there are three categories of questions and you can anticipate that these same questions are going to come again in the future.

Well now you can create templated answers, anticipating when these questions are going to be asked again in the future. Instead of having you or your support team or whoever's responsible for answering these questions type out those answers again, you can have templates created or create an FAQ section and now you've got something that's already done for you.

It's already completely systemized, so when this action takes place your company is set up to automatically handle that action and move on. It doesn't interrupt what you're currently doing, the growth you're currently working on.

The more you do this, the more you find processes and systemize things you're already doing, the greater the asset base you build in your business and the more money you're going to be able to make, because you're handling more things. The more you can handle, the more money you can make.

So always be on the lookout for things that you're doing that are of a repetitive nature that you can systemize or put into some template of some sort.

Building Your Network

Finally, building your network. When it comes to business development, it's impossible to develop your business and to become successful as an entrepreneur if you're not expanding your network.

The problem is a lot of people do it the wrong way.

They go into these online social networks, like LinkedIn, and they just start asking for people to help them, or they go to a live event and they talk all about themselves.

The key to building your network is to reach out and connect with other people, and the best way to do that is to meet people for the sake of meeting them and take interest in who they are and their lives.

Not just what they do for work, but in their personal lives: Where they live, how many kids they have, where they grew up, some of the things they do outside of business, some of the projects they may be working on that have nothing to do with making money.

You can connect with people at all different kinds of levels.

I've talked to a number of different entrepreneurs. Some of their best partners, some of the best people in their network, are people they connected with outside of business. Maybe they played on the same sports team together or maybe they were interested in the same kind of hobby.

Meeting at that level, they had a common connection, a common bond, and then it just so happened that the business connections flowed naturally out of that.

When you go into a networking event or into a networking situation with the goal and determination of, "I've just got to build my network and I have to find as many people who can make more money as possible", you're doing it the wrong way.

You're actually going to repel people. They're not going to be interested in talking to you, because they'll see you're only in this for the business side of it.

You're only in it to make contacts, to maybe grow your prospect list and there's nothing they're really going to gain from it intellectually or even in a relationship capacity.

Always think of meeting people for the sake of meeting them, and then just let it flow naturally from there. You'll be amazed at the amount of connections you'll make, even with just one good relationship.

So, treat those relationships really, really well and build your network tactfully, focusing on the person first. If you do that well and you do everything I've talked about in this chapter, then your business development is in the right path for success.

Exercises

Let's quickly talk about some business development exercises that you can put into play right now.

List three money-making skills that bring in money on a regular basis and brainstorm how you can strengthen them. You're already doing well with these, they're bringing revenue into your business. How can you take that further? What can you do to enhance the skill? What can you do to find more customers who will pay for that skill? Think of all the different ways you can transform this into even more opportunity for your business.

List three money-draining tasks. These are tasks that actually cost your business. Things that you're doing on a regular basis that are preventing you from spending time on those other three that are making you the money. Brainstorm ways you can remove them, either through systemizing, delegating, outsourcing, hiring, removing them altogether in some cases, but sit down and think of them at a detailed level so you can remove them.

Doing these two tasks will be hugely transformational to your business development.

2. CONFIDENCE

This chapter is about one of the most important topics any of us can learn, and that is self-confidence. Not just self-confidence when it comes to operating your business, but self-confidence in general in your life.

If you can become more confident, you can have a happier life.

And I think you already know this at a gut level, but have you ever actually sat down and asked yourself what confidence actually means?

You see a lot of people looking at a certain confident person and maybe even admiring them from afar saying, "Wow, look at his/her confidence", but they never actually sit down and think, "What does confidence mean?" Well, let's talk about it.

Confidence is really a state of mind. It's the way you see the world, and your perceptions will actually shape how you feel about the world

But it's not just a state of mind; it's actually a physical state. It's something we can describe physically, a sensation we feel in our body.

The thing is, confidence is absolutely required if you want to come up with the right ideas to succeed, if you want to make intelligent plans for success in your life and your business, and most importantly if you want to be able to follow through on the action that is required to succeed.

Think about it. Let's say you're just starting a business right now or maybe you've already been in business for a few years and something happens. There's some kind of problem you need to deal with, and you approach that problem from a position of lack of confidence or fear.

Are you going to have access to the same ideas? Are you going to come up with approaches that are going to be the same as if you were feeling very confident or powerful or fearless about the situation?

Of course, you know the answer is no. If you're feeling unconfident, if you're feeling weary or fearful of the situation, of the problem, and there's even an ounce of doubt in your mind that you're going to be able to handle this, you will simply not have access to ideas or trains of thought that will help you get out of this problem as effectively as if you were to approach the problem with forced confidence, with a high degree of self-reliance and fearlessness.

We need to work on our ability to get into a confident state of mind but also into a confident physical state so that we literally feel like we can take on any problem that comes our way.

If we can do that, if we can get our mindset to a place where we suddenly begin to feel like, "I can handle this. I can think rationally about this problem and think back to other times in my life where I was also faced with some big stuff in the past and I got through it."

You can start building that up and when you start developing a higher level of confidence and you're looking at a problem, now you can go to part B and start making intelligent plans for success.

Because you're starting to feel better about the problem, your plans will start to look better. As the plans look better, you start looking at the actions required to make that plan come to fruition and you're able to actually follow through on the action because you're feeling better about yourself and your ability to take on whatever this problem may be.

Sometimes, let's face it, there are going to be huge problems we have to deal with in business. A lot of times, these problems may force us to confront somebody, to get into a fearful situation or something that makes us feel bad or something where we just want to run away scared.

But because we force ourselves to go through that, we can dedicate new levels of confidence and we can actually acquire confidence that we can build moving forward.

You must always carry with you and know at a gut level that you can build confidence.

Myths

There are some really pervasive myths that hurt a lot of people. One of the myths is they look at other people who are more confident than them and think to themselves, "Wow, that person is so lucky. Look how confident they are."

They believe this other myth is true, that confidence comes naturally. That may be true to a degree, but it's certainly not entirely true. Confidence can be developed, and until you accept that, until you realize that, you'll never be able to actually develop your own confidence.

If you're honest with yourself right now and you look at areas in your life that are lacking, you can very likely tie that back to a lack of confidence in some area of your life, in some mindset that you're constantly bringing up where you have a lack of confidence.

You have confidence. Even if you're the type of person where you think you're lacking, you have confidence. It just may not be confidence where you want it.

Think about things that you're already proficient at: Walking, running, driving. There was a time in your life where you were not good at those things, assuming you do those things.

Assuming you do these things, think back to when you were younger and you couldn't do them proficiently. You were not confident. Luckily for us at the time, when we were learning things like walking, we were a little bit more fearless back then and we just kept doing it until we got proficient at it.

Driving is a little bit better of an example, because we do that when we're a little bit older.

We start off driving, especially if you want to learn manual transmission versus automatic, you can have a very, very low level of confidence because there is so much going on.

But as you practice it, as you develop proficiency for this, your confidence for that thing grows.

And so just looking at that process, the way we as humans interact with new things in our lives and the way we develop our proficiency, the proficiency leads to confidence.

That's all you need to realize here, is your lack of confidence is for just one reason. You have not worked on developing your confidence in that area.

So maybe you lack confidence in confronting people that are giving you a problem. Maybe you lack confidence in selling. You know you're good at what you do. The service you provide or the products you create are very valuable. You know that you can help your customers.

But when it comes time to close the deal, you freeze because you lack the confidence. Now you can remind yourself that, "I just have not developed my confidence in selling. It doesn't mean I will never be a confident salesperson; it just means I have not developed it yet."

That is sometimes all you need to realize to begin your journey towards a higher level of confidence, in whatever area you're currently deficient at.

The Confidence Formula

Let's look at the confidence formula.

First of all, you need to do a reality check, and you have to focus on different areas of your life right now where you may be lacking in confidence. Ask the truthful question: Where am I confidence-wise and where do I lack it?

Maybe your confidence is decent when it comes to writing down the reasons why your products are good, but when it comes to having a conversation with somebody about why your product is so good and why they should buy it, that's where your confidence lacks.

Make sure you understand at a detailed level, the exact implications of your confidence and exactly where it's at.

Then, in the areas where you are confident, let's say you can do a pretty good job of writing out all the features and benefits and all the reasons why your product is good, you can write that down with no problem, then inflate that.

Really build it up in your mind and congratulate yourself for being that confident and for having the awareness that you are that good and realize, "I do have confidence when it comes to writing down the features and benefits of my service."

From there, you need to find the implications of the lack of confidence, in detail.

So, "Yes, I'm good at writing it, but I'm not good at speaking these features and benefits. I'm not good at discussing why somebody should buy this. I can't close a deal in person."

List all of the implications. What is happening, as a result of you not being able to do this?

Let's say most of your deals come in through face-to-face selling. Well, the implications of that are you're not making very much money. You're not able to sell as much of what you should be selling, in order to be successful in business.

Maybe it's causing you to do less work. Maybe it's causing you to shy away from finding new prospects, because you dread the idea of actually finding somebody who's interested in buying from you.

List out each and every implication of you not being confident in that particular area of your life.

Next, you need to go and find somebody who is really, really good at what you want to be good at.

In the previous example, there is no shortage of people in this world who are very good and confident at selling face-to-face. There are people who can sell from a stage or a platform. There are people who can go into a boardroom full of executives and close the place down and get them to buy everything in their arsenal.

There are amazing salespeople out there, and you need to develop relationships or at least study people who are already good at that so you can start seeing what it is that gives them confidence and what they do to be so good at that.

Then, create a plan.

"My confidence is lacking, I want to get to a higher level of confidence. What is my plan to begin building proficiencies so that I can become more confident? More confident tomorrow, even more confident next week, even more confident next month and then by a year from now I may have totally obliterated all of my lack of confidence in this area and I may be the best face-to-face salesperson you have ever seen."

But it all comes down to this confidence formula:

- Doing a **reality check** of where you're at.

- **Inflating the confidence you already have,** to prove to yourself that you have it.

- **Find the implications** of not developing the confidence, so you can get mad at yourself.

- **Find role models** who already do a good job at it, so you can study them and create a plan to be more like them in your own unique way.

Exercises

Now let's talk about a couple of exercises you can work on now, that will help you to develop your confidence now and over time.

First, log your victories.

This is incredibly powerful. I want you to begin today, and every day moving forward, to build an growing list of successes and wins and victories, whatever you want to call it, that you can review on an ongoing basis.

This is done really well with something like Evernote, or you can even do it in a notepad with pen and paper. The key is that you do it.

Every time something happens, whether it's something really, really small like a small testimonial email that you received from a customer, or it can be huge, like an award you received, log that victory.

Write about it. Describe it in as much detail as possible so that you can go back and when your confidence is low in the future, you can read this growing log and build that confidence back up in an instant.

Then, go and do a reality check. Do a full inventory on where you are and where you are not confident, as it stands today, and be completely honest with yourself.

You'll see areas where you have an abundance of confidence and you feel really great about yourself, but you'll also see the opposite. Areas where you need to work on your confidence, you need to develop it and improve it.

But based on everything we've gone over, you can start taking action on that and moving them from one column over to the other. But until you log it all, until you have a full inventory, you can't really do this effectively.

Do your reality check, as well as your logging of victories, and you'll be well on your way to being a much more confident person.

3. CONSTANT IMPROVEMENT

This chapter is all about constant improvement, and I believe this is an area that a lot of entrepreneurs and business owners take for granted, or in some cases, don't even think about at all.

I want to shine some light on this and inspire you to think about it, not right now only but all of the time and show you how you can bring the idea and the philosophy of constant improvement into your world, so that you can be more successful in your business.

It all starts with this: Real happiness comes from mastery.

I want you to think about that idea for a minute. Think about some of the times in your life where you felt the most alive, and specifically in business, the times that were the most exciting for you.

Yes, it's great when a big paycheck comes in, when a lot of money comes in, but some of the most invigorating times, especially when you take a poll of entrepreneurs, the most invigorating, enlightening, exciting times come from those moments where they have truly conquered something. They truly mastered something.

For a professional speaker, it might be the first time they delivered a speech and got a standing ovation. For an author, it might be getting that first book published and making your first sale.

It could be anything, but the idea of starting off small, starting off with a limited skill set, developing your skills over time and eventually becoming extremely proficient at something is one of the most rewarding experiences you can ever have in your life.

The really cool part about this is as you develop competency for something and as you become a master at it, that process never ends. You can never completely master something.

It's a very, very interesting paradoxical thing, when you think about it. You can always get better at whatever it is that you're doing, and that's why you see some of the best people in the world at their craft continue to work on it, continue to develop and hone their skills.

They're almost addicted to this growth process that they get into.

Realize that real happiness is going to come from your mastery more than it's going to come from any other format of business.

What are you mastering? That's the question you want to ask yourself.

Patience

I also want to get you thinking about the idea of patience. Patience is a lost art form.

There are so few people who are willing to go through the almost painful experience of spending the hours, putting the time in required to become good at something, to constantly improve something, to master something.

It's a painful thing to do. Let's face it. When you first start something, I don't care if you're learning how to play the guitar or you have no tech experience and you want to learn how to develop websites, all of these things have this massive list of skill that you must develop and the initial phases are painful.

A huge degree of patience is required, and that patience is often what's lacking in most people and that's what causes people to abandon the art of mastery altogether.

Realizing that patience is one of your biggest virtues, it's one of the most important things you have to embrace and hone into your life.

And it doesn't mean you're not going to get frustrated; it means you understand the process that patience is required, that, "I am going to feel frustration, that I may even actually feel pain or anxiety because I have to face this thing that I'm not good at yet and go through that really awkward phase to a point where I finally start to catch it."

When you realize that, when you realize that patience is a lost art form and that few people are willing to do it, it makes it easier for you to persist through those difficult times, because you remind yourself that so few other people are going to do it.

By the time you get through it, it's going to be so worth it because you've past the test that 99 out of 100 people will not pass.

What is your level of patience right now? Again, it doesn't mean you're not going to experience frustration or yell a bunch of curse words at the wall, whatever it is.

You're going to do that, but you're also going to go through that process, remembering that if you persist, and more importantly if you're patient enough to get through that to a point where you finally make that breakthrough, that's when things start beginning to turn around for you and you're committed to the philosophy of constant improvement.

Now, if you think back to business development when we talked about focusing in on one skill or a small skill set of things that you do naturally well, that people pay you for your expertise for, if you've done that correctly and now you come to this section when we start talking about constant improvement, it doesn't get any better than this.

You are getting paid to get good at your passions. Constant improvement will just come naturally to you, because there are people out there paying you to do this thing and here you are going through the mastery phases, going through that phase of patience and persistence to just get better at something that you already want to be doing anyways.

This is where things become really sweet. You become a person who makes a lot of money and you're really, really happy in making that money.

If you don't do the first part, if you don't hone in on the things that you want to do and want to master, then it's impossible to get to the phase of getting paid to get good at your passions.

I'm sure you would agree that nothing really trumps this. If you can get paid to get good at something you already want to do, that's pretty awesome.

Finally, make it a game or a challenge to improve every single day. Try to beat your record.

For me personally, when I really commit to my fitness and I want to increase my cardiovascular strength, when I'm doing a certain length run and I time it, I know that I want to beat my time even if it's by one second.

I'm driven and motivated and inspired to beat that time I did the day before.

Or if there's a certain product I sold and it sold X amount of dollars, I want to see if I can do X times 2, or even X plus 1 if I have to. Just beat it by a little bit.

The fact that you can see the results and you can see the increase is huge motivational fuel to do it again and to persist through and to actually get you through that patience phase that you know you're going to need.

If you turn it into a game where you keep score and you track things and you see you're increasing and improving every day, it makes it that much easier.

See it as a game, not as a chore, and you're going to love it. And the idea of self-improvement, constant improvement, is going to come naturally to you.

Exercises

Here are a couple of exercises you can do right now to begin working on and honing your ability to have constant improvement and focus on doing that on an ongoing basis.

First, you need to book a time where you're going to dedicate some focused attention to perfecting and mastering your craft on a daily basis.

Some people like to get up an hour early and dedicate that first hour of their day to this specific form of improving themselves, of developing their craft, developing their mastery around whatever topic it is that's important to them.

It could be at the end of the day. It could be on your lunch break, or it might be at random times throughout the week.

The key is that you do this and you do it every single day. I can almost guarantee you that as you start doing it, you'll start dedicating more and more time to this on a daily and monthly and even yearly basis.

Next, you want to create a log. This can be a journal that you write in or a notebook you have online or on your phone, where you can start tracking the progress of your improvement.

You can describe how your skill is developing, how you feel about it, what you've been able to do today versus where you were last week and where you're going in the future.

This brings an awareness of how you've been improving and it fuels that mode that you get into when you want to improve even further.

It makes this constant improvement methodology a lot easier for you to embrace, when you can visually see track points and case studies along the way of how you have been improving your craft.

But you can't do that unless you log it, so begin logging it today and constant improvement will be part of your life moving forward.

4. DRIVING FORCE

Now we're going to discuss a huge topic, a topic that not a lot of people ever consider, even though there are plenty of entrepreneurs out there, but only a few of them really think about this and that is your driving force.

Why you're in business. The reason why you do what you do.

There has to be meaning in why you run your business and why you are an entrepreneur.

You have to have a purpose for what you do. Having a purpose and identifying your meaning is an absolute must, if you really want to succeed.

If you want to be able to persist through all of the problems, the relentless issues that you're going to be dealing with as an entrepreneur, something else has to be driving you.

It can't be just about the money. We all need money.

I know that you need money, you know that I need money and we'd be lying to ourselves if we thought money wasn't important. It's important. We can't have anything in our lives without it.

However, money cannot be the only motivation. We need to ask ourselves, "What makes me come alive?"

What makes you as an individual have drive, have passion, have purpose behind your actions, so that you're not just going through the motions on a day-to-day basis, building a big checklist of to-do's for your day and methodically clicking them off one by one, without any passion or excitement for what you do.

You need to know what makes you come alive, what makes you become passionate and feel what you're doing and feel good about what you're doing, beyond the money.

For each and every person it's going to be different, and for each and every person there are probably a variety of things that cause them to have meaning or that develop their why, the reason why they're in business to begin with.

Examples

We're just going to go through a few examples here, and often these will apply to many, many people, although it's not limited to this list. But let's talk about them.

First, to be the best in the world at what you do.

How cool would that be, to know that whatever vocation you've chosen, whatever business you've decided to go into, how awesome would it be to know that you are among the best in the world at what you do? Top 1%.

In any vocation you can think of, there are hundreds of thousands, probably millions of people trying to do it, and you're one of the top 1%. The reward that you get from that, from knowing that you are the best at what you do is sometimes all people need to drive them forward.

To lead and inspire an audience.

Some people get so much meaning, knowing that others are following them and looking to them for advice and looking to them for power and for confidence in their lives.

Maybe you thrive on knowing that others are looking to you as a source of power in their lives, and by operating your business and operating yourself in certain ways, you can actually be that leader and that inspiration for those people.

To pave a new way for your children.

A lot of entrepreneurs right now are doing this exact thing. A lot of us were raised in an environment where we were taught to go to school for one particular area and then to get a job and then to focus on building your typical career path in that job, waiting until the time you retire.

It doesn't matter if you like it or you don't like it, this is what you're supposed to do and this is what we've been taught to do. We all know that's no way to live your life, especially if you're miserable.

By becoming an entrepreneur, you're paving an entirely new way for your children. You're creating a new way of looking at life, a more empowering way of looking at life. Your children are having something modeled for them that was never modeled for you, and you're literally breaking a pattern.

For some people, that's all they focus on and their entire business fuel, their fuel to succeed in business comes from this need to change their ways so that their children can have a new outlook on life.

Becoming totally self-reliant and independent.

This is when you don't need a boss and an employer to give you money so that you can show up somewhere and get a certified payment in your bank account.

On the opposite end, you embrace the uncertainty and you're okay with the fact that you don't know if you're going to get paid until you deliver. But you're okay with that, because it develops you as a person and now you're on the hook for becoming totally self-reliant.

Now, anything can happen in the world around you and you develop the confidence over time as a business owner, to know that, "It doesn't matter what happens; I'm self-reliant. I'm independent and I'm capable of handling it myself. I don't need anybody to help me out."

That is a huge driving force for a lot of people.

To prove something to yourself, or even better, to prove to someone else.

I've heard of business people whose entire motivation was to prove someone wrong because they were doubted in some way or slighted by someone else and they became indignant and angry and mad that that person would doubt them.

That fueled them way past all these other entrepreneurs competing with them and they became the best at what they did, just because they had to prove someone wrong. They were angry that somebody doubted them.

Has somebody slighted you or doubted you? Maybe your own mind has doubted you and your capabilities to do something with your life and you need to prove to yourself or to that other person that you are capable of doing this. That can be your drive or your motivation.

Solving a huge problem in the world or an injustice that you're seeing.

Most people just complain that the government's not solving these problems. Maybe you're the kind of person that says, "Well, nobody's solving this problem, so I'm going to step up and solve it. By creating this business, by being an entrepreneur and by raising capital and becoming worth more and more money, I can now be in a position to have enough power to solve this problem."

Rather than waiting for someone else to solve it, you're going to solve it. And in order for you to solve it, you have to be successful in business.

Maybe that's your driving force. Maybe that's your why.

To face the fears that have held you back.

A lot of people stay in a job that they hate because they're just too fearful to even think about what it might be like to have to go at it alone.

Maybe you're just so sick and tired of all the negative implications that happen when you live from a position of fear, that it's time to stomp on those fears and solve them once in for all.

You overcoming your fear is what drives you to success as an entrepreneur.

These are just some typical examples, and I'm sure at least one or two of these are true for you, but it's really, really important that you get in touch with them.

Exercises

Let's talk about a couple of exercises for developing your driving force.

First, brainstorm issues that bother you. Anything in this world, anything about the way you've been living your life, or like we talked about earlier, things that you see happening in the world around you, anything that really bothers you, list them down and then rank them.

You might be bothered by how timid and nervous and shy you are around other people that are more aggressive and you want to solve that problem.

Or you may be bothered by some kind of injustice, like we talked about earlier, that's happening in the world.

Brainstorm and think about all the things that bother you and rank them so that you know what charges you, from the highest to the lowest level.

From there, looking at all these different things that bother you and that you want to solve and create your driving force, your "Why statement," so that as you build your business and as you face these mountains of to-do's and these new things you have to develop and difficult situations you're going to face, you can always come back to this reason why.

Why are you doing this in the first place? Why did you create this business? Why are you an entrepreneur?

If you get intimately familiar with your driving force, or your "Why," then as you face these difficult situations they become easier and easier and your proficiency grows higher and you become better at

**doing what it is that you want to be doing because
of this statement.**

Create your "Why statement," right now, brainstorm all
of these things and then as you move forward your
business will just get easier and easier for you to
expand and grow.

5. ENERGY MANAGEMENT

You cannot have any degree of success as an entrepreneur unless you are a high-energy person, unless you manage your energy.

Realize that your energy levels will ultimately determine your success in business.

Take a minute just to think about this for a second. Think about any successful entrepreneur that you've either studied from afar or even met in person and looked at what they live like, how they operate.

Are these people what you consider low-energy, unproductive people? Probably not.

These are people that are driven, they're passionate, they have a high level of energy on an ongoing basis.

One of the root causes of their success is because they have a high level of energy, and that high level of energy connects them to better ideas, to more inspiring thoughts that make them take more action, that gives them even more energy and it becomes this positive cycle.

Knowing that your energy levels will determine your success, you need to make it your mission to become a high-energy person on an ongoing basis. In order to do that, you need to understand how energy works.

How Energy Works

The basic premise is that energy flows in rhythms.

Even the people that you look at right now and you might think, "Wow, they've got a lot of energy and I don't", energy flows in rhythms. Those people, while they may appear to be high energy, they also experience lows.

They're not always at a level 10. They do hit their level zeros and ones, and there's times where they feel like passing out, too. They've just become better at managing it.

Understanding that energy flows in rhythms and what to do about it is very important. When to take a break.

How long you should focus and how long you should be detaching from it.

There's a book by Tony Schwartz called "The Power of Full Engagement," that actually dives deep into this idea of maximizing your energy by having intense periods of focused concentration but then deliberately taking breaks, to allow yourself time to recover.

This is all about rhythms of energy. How your energy flows. You need to become intimately aware of your energy patterns.

In order to do that, you have to become conscious of your energy levels:

- What is your energy like on a daily basis?

- Do you have your most energy in the morning and then it kind of dwindles as your day goes along?

- Do you start off really slow and then build up momentum, only to have it leave later on and come back in the evenings?

These flows are partly particular to you and to your schedule, but they're also a rhythm that you've been living with right now.

Just becoming conscious of what your energy has been like in your life up to this point is very important, but you also need to realize that you can change it and you can deliberately create new energy patterns in your life.

Honestly, it all starts with changing your beliefs about low energy.

I'm sure you've seen this in your life as well. It happens with kids all the time, where the kid can be sitting there on the couch and bored out of their mind and they say they feel like sleeping, they have no energy or desire to do anything at all, especially if you ask them to do a chore.

But then you suddenly introduce the idea of doing something fun, like going to an amusement park or going out to get a treat. These kids are suddenly jolted to life. They have this explosion of energy, and they've gone from a level 1 or 2 up to a level 10.

The same thing can happen with adults.

You're sitting there, you don't feel like doing anything because maybe you're depressed about the stack of work that you've been looking at and suddenly a state change happens where something new is introduced, a show comes on that you're interested in or somebody calls that you haven't talked to in a long time and they have something exciting to share with you. Now your energy levels have suddenly shot up to a new level.

You're not locked into these low levels of energy. You're not stuck there. You can immediately go from a low to a high by changing your focus.

But a lot of people don't believe that's possible, so it's important that you change your beliefs about low energy and just realize that there are going to be triggers that you can activate that take you from a low to a high.

This is especially important for entrepreneurs, because it's not always going to be convenient to have a high level of energy.

You might feel really, really terrible and suddenly you need to be on because there's an opportunity to make money or to do something that's going to create success in your business and you need to be able to activate high energy in that moment, even though you may not feel like it.

You have to be able to challenge your beliefs about your current levels of low energy.

Lack of Sleep

But you also need to challenge your beliefs about lack of sleep. You may not want to hear this, but the truth of the matter is that most successful entrepreneurs, especially people in the early phases, year 1, year 2, year 3, there are going to be times where you have to sacrifice sleep.

You might not want to hear this, but for the most part this is true.

There are going to be times when you're going to be putting in 17, 18, 19-hour days, maybe there are days you don't sleep at all and you have these tapes playing in your mind saying, "Oh my gosh, you shouldn't be doing this. You need sleep. You're going to get sick."

You need to be able to challenge your beliefs about lack of sleep, because there are people who have gone days without sleep and they were perfectly fine because they made up their mind that this is something they needed to do.

It is a state of mind.

I'm not here telling you that you can live a perfectly healthy, balanced life by sleeping two hours a night. That's not what I'm telling you.

What I'm telling you is challenge your belief about lack of sleep, because there will be times, especially in the beginning phases of entrepreneurship, where you're going to have to push your limits and sleep less than you've been accustomed to in the past.

There is a part of your mind that is going to become fearful, and you cannot allow this fear to take you over. You need to take a position that says, "I'm okay without sleep. It may feel uncomfortable, my eyes might get heavy and tired and my energy might feel low, but I'm going to persist through this because plenty of other people have done it and they did not get some kind of terminal disease by sleeping less. They just worked through that problem or worked through that scenario and they got through to the end."

Realize that lack of sleep is probably going to happen to you at some point in the earlier phases of business and it may not feel great, and you may even get run down or maybe you even get a little bit sick, but you'll recover.

You'll use time to get some extra sleep and get back on your feet.

This is more about fear than it is anything else. Don't allow these preconceived beliefs that you need eight hours a night or else you're going to be really, really unhealthy. Don't let that control you.

This is all about energy management, and more importantly, taking control of your time and your life.

Monitor Impacts to Your Energy

You also need to start monitoring how certain foods or behaviors or business activities or thought patterns impact your energy.

All these things, they seem like a random collection of things, but they can all have a direct impact on your energy.

If you have a huge plate of pasta at lunch and then you feel really full for the next two hours and you can barely do any work, you're doing two minutes of productive work in those next two hours, then maybe you should skip the pasta and eat something a little healthier.

Maybe there's a certain business activity, like accounting, filling in spreadsheets, that causes you to feel really, really low energy.

You can begin to anticipate certain activities or behaviors.

Maybe when you get into this mindset about worrying about the numbers or the books, that causes your energy to go down.

When you monitor how these different things impact your energy, then you can start becoming conscious, like I said earlier, and say, "Oh, look what's happening here. My energy is starting to dip. Where have I been focusing? Okay, time to do something about it."

Exercises

There are a couple of exercises that I want you to do today, to begin taking control of your energy levels, to begin managing your energy.

First, create a log. Create a log of different foods, events, thought patterns and tasks that seem to zap your energy, that seem to put you at a low, that make you feel like, "Oh man, why did I get in business to begin with? I just want to go to bed right now."

Start logging what it is that causes you to get to that level.

Then, figure out an antidote. What's the opposite of it? What's your equivalent of being a little kid and your parent coming in when you're really tired or you've been given a task you didn't want to do and suddenly saying, "Hey, if you get this done we can go to the amusement park", and now your energy level is at a 10 again.

You have antidotes that you can begin to bring into your life. You just have to figure out what they are. What snaps you from a level zero to a level 10? Or maybe more subtly from a level 3 to a 7, because all you need is a 7 right now.

But figure out how to increase your energy when you need it, so that you can use it as you need it, and then when your energy levels are low and it's time for a recovery you can take it. And when it's not time for a recovery, you have strategies to get through it, until it's a reasonable time for you to take a break and to relax.

Use this now, become a master of your energy and watch your business grow.

6. DEALING WITH FEAR

You know, just by looking at the title here, that if you do not deal with fear that your level of success will always be capped.

I want to discuss how to deal with, how to conquer, how to work through our fears so that they no longer stop us and we can reach whatever level of success we determine we want in our lives.

Start by realizing that the average person in our world, when we look around us, is fear-based. Look at your neighborhood or your circle of friends or even in your family and look at the moves and decisions and ideas people carry around with them.

Most people are fear-based.

If you look at somebody that has a really terrible job and they've never done anything about it, they're fear-based. They're staying there because they're too afraid to do anything about it because they're afraid of what might happen if they quit and go out on their own.

If you look at somebody who lets people walk all over them because they're too afraid to confront those people and deal with the problem and so they get stuck in this prison of effectively their own fears because they worry about what might happen if they actually take some corrective action to deal with the problem.

These are just two small examples, but this is stuff that plagues people in our everyday lives when we look around us. People are fear-based.

If you want to succeed as an entrepreneur, you must overcome this. You cannot be a fear-based individual. You cannot make decisions that are fear-based.

How do you move yourself out of that trap?

Become Aware

It starts by becoming aware. Becoming aware of how your fears are holding you back, how certain fears are creeping into your life and stopping you from taking actions that you probably know you need to be doing to be successful but you're not doing them because of these fears and because of something you're probably imagining is going to happen. Whether it will or not is yet to be determined, because you haven't taken the action.

But your fear of it happening is stopping you dead in your tracks and it's perpetuating a cycle of failure, because you keep doing the same things over and over again that are producing these results that you don't want.

Becoming aware of how your fears are holding you back is very, very important, but it also requires that you become aware of what fears exist in general.

What kind of fears do you have?

- Are you fearful of confronting somebody?

- Are you fearful of making a presentation?

- Are you fearful of putting your work out for scrutinizing or criticism because you just don't think you can handle other peoples' negative opinions of you?

There is probably a laundry list of things that every entrepreneur has to deal with, when it comes to fears, that hold them back.

But until they look these fears in the face and start understanding the implications of them, of what it's actually costing them to invest in these fears, they never do anything about it.

Start thinking about that. What kind of fears do you have? More importantly, how are those fears actually blocking you?

Study Your Fear

You can do this by studying your fear, and that starts with decomposing your fear into the root cause or the origin.

Ultimately, you want to understand why you have the fear to begin with, at least to the best of your ability.

Let's use an example of public speaking, which is a common one. Most people are afraid to speak in front of a group of people, but they just leave it at that.

They just say, "Well, I'm afraid of public speaking", and they just don't do it.

But let's assume you're a successful entrepreneur or aspiring to be one, and you want to deal with this problem once and for all.

So you look at the problem. "Okay, the problem is I'm afraid of speaking. Why? I might get up there and forget my lines and it's going to look really, really bad. I'm going to look like a fool."

Have you looked like a fool before in your life? Have you dealt with problems where you put yourself in a situation where you couldn't deliver? Were you able to recover from that?

If you're honest with yourself, you know the answer is yes. You've messed up in the past and you've recovered from it. Maybe your ego was a little bruised, but time heals most wounds and you dealt with it.

The ultimate fear in this situation is messing up and looking a little foolish for a while. Well hey, you're an entrepreneur. You better be able to handle looking like a fool once in a while, because you're going to make mistakes. That's just the nature of the game.

Not just in entrepreneurship, but in life.

However, if you don't actually do this exercise, if you just say, "I'm fearful of public speaking", and don't take it a step further, then you'll never do the action of public speaking.

You just won't, because you don't understand the root cause of the fear. But if you take it a little further and rationalize a bit, it makes more sense.

Then you can go to step two here, which is studying your fear responses.

So you're about to deliver the speech and you say to yourself, "Man, I'm really scared." Well, what does that actually mean? What physically happens to you?

Does it mean your chest is pounding, your hands are shaking, you're sweating a little bit? Everybody had different physical sensations when they're fearful.

But actually studying it and realizing what the fear response manifests like in your body can help you deal with it, and it can help you anticipate it in the future.

If you're feeling fearful now and these are the symptoms you're seeing, the next time you feel fearful you actually realize, "Hey, I'm getting the same symptoms. This is just fear. Did I deal with it last time? Yes, I did. That's the basis for success. I can do it again."

It's really interesting. I've heard Tony Robbins tell the story of Bruce Springsteen talking about how excited he gets before a concert and he explains the physical sensations of his chest being tight and all these different things going on in his body, and to him that signifies to his brain that he's ready.

Another artist who had the exact same sensations, whose career actually faltered for a while because she thought she was dealing with stage fright, experienced the exact same things.

Bruce Springsteen learned to interpret those physical sensations as excitement, where this other person was interpreting it as fear-based.

It's neither here nor there. It's the fact that one person decided to work through it and go with it and make the best of it, and the other person let it stop them.

Finally, recall situations where your fear was exaggerated, which is almost always.

Going back to the fear of public speaking, you may feel the physical sensations like you're about to die because you're just so scared to speak. Is that a reasonable state of physical being to be in, just because you're delivering a speech?

You know the answer is no. It's not really reasonable for you to feel that much terror just because you're getting up in front of a group of people to speak. They're not going to slay you or throw bows and arrows at you because you gave a bad speech. Yet, your body feels as though your life is being threatened.

It's not really realistic, yet our fear exaggerates how intense it really is for us. That's why you want to study your fears.

Anytime you have something that is fearful and that is actually blocking you from taking actions that are going to help you succeed, this is a process that you can go through to actually come to grips with what the fear really is all about.

Develop a Hate of Fear

Next, you need to develop a hate of fear so that you can act in spite of it. This quote is beautiful: "**True courage is not the absence of fear but the willingness to proceed in spite of it.**"

You might look around at some really successful entrepreneurs and think to yourself, "Wow, look at what they can handle. Look at the things they do. They're getting on TV and they're speaking to thousands of people. I could never do that. They have so much natural courage and they have fewer fears than me."

That's just wrong. It's not true. Those people have learned how to act in spite of their fears.

Some of the most successful people are actually incredibly nervous. They hate getting up in front of crowds, but they do it anyways because they've conditioned themselves to have true courage, to act in spite of fear.

Get out of this mindset that says, "Well, I'm fearful and they're not." Everybody is fearful. The people that you aspire to be like have just learned how to deal with it and move through those fears. Maybe the fears don't grip them as strongly as they used to, because they made a habit of working through it.

Now you have to make the same habit as well, in your life.

Exercises

Let's do that with the following exercises.

First, make a list of anything that you are nervous, afraid or fearful of. Make as long of a list as possible so that you can become consciously aware of all of your fears.

Next, make another list of how these fears prevent you from getting what you want. This will actually make you angry, and it should, because you're building up this huge pile of fears and they're stopping you from getting these things you really want in your business or maybe your life as well.

Finally, make a commitment to act in spite of these fears. You're going to do it. You're going to feel the fear and do it anyway, which is the title of a book but it's beautiful advice.

You're not going to worry about getting rid of these sensations of anxiety and things that you feel when you're fearful. You're just going to realize that they're going to happen but you're still going to do it anyway.

Once you make a habit of doing that, you have conquered your fear, you've managed your fear, now you can begin to take all kinds of actions to grow your business and become that much more successful as an entrepreneur.

7. FOCUS YOUR MIND

If you really want success, if you want to do something that's going to elevate you to the next level and do something that the average person just isn't doing, this topic is key. That is, your ability to focus your mind.

In today's world, there have never been more distractions for human beings to deal with. We are constantly being bombarded with instant messages, text messages, checking our email, phones ringing, you name it.

Our focus and our attention is being diverted in 100 different directions at all times, and this has a huge negative impact especially on entrepreneurs who need to be extremely productive and extremely efficient, if they want to build a successful business.

If you want to build a successful business and if that's your goal and that's what you're doing right now, then you already know instinctively that focus is going to be one of your absolute, most critical pieces to that success puzzle.

You have to start by realizing what focus is.

What is Focus?

Focus is actually a mental faculty. When I say mental faculty, I mean it's one of the ways in which our minds think. It is the will of our mind to have sustained concentration, to think about and focus on and take action on one thing for an extended period of time so that we can build this momentum, this feeling good about a particular task.

I'm sure you've been in that flow state before, where you forced yourself to do nothing else except this one task.

It could be writing, it could be recording something, it could be manual labor, but you focused on it for a while, you started to develop some momentum and before you knew it you were heads down and really cranking out great material, whatever it was.

That is the power of focus. The problem is, we rarely these days give ourselves a chance to build that momentum anymore.

We might get 5 or 10 minutes into a task and we allow the phone ring to stop us or we allow the sound of a new email coming in to divert our attention to something new and we never reap the rewards of this incredibly powerful momentum that we get when we focus.

It's just like when you're outside on a sunny day and you can get a suntan, but at the same time if somebody took a magnifying glass and took those same sun rays but focused and harnessed them into a single beam of light on your skin, it would burn you.

It's the exact same energy. Our mind has the exact same energy, but when we focus it on one thing we can have a far more powerful affect.

That is the essence of what we're going for. To reach the pinnacle of success as an entrepreneur, you need to have laser-like focus on the things that you need to be doing to grow your business.

Unless you're focusing on those, your attention is being diverted in a million different directions and you'll never make the progress that you need to make to reach the really big and lofty goals that you're likely setting already in your life.

Realize that focus is actually a skill. It's a skill and a habit.

If you work on your focus on a daily basis, you can get into the habit of being really good at focusing on things and it can be deliberately strengthened. But unless you make the choice to deliberately strengthen it, you're never going to actually realize that benefit.

So, realize it's a skill and then realize that you can do something about it.

Identify What Breaks Your Focus

But you have to start by identifying things. Most importantly, identify what breaks or interrupts your focus, as it stands today.

Maybe you sat down this morning to read a couple of articles that were relevant to your business and you couldn't even get through the first half of the article without being interrupted or distracted by something, let's say a text message, one of the most popular interruptions that exist.

You need to start identifying in your life where all of your interruptions exist and what breaks your focus, and you can start making a list of those things.

But even just becoming consciously aware of how your focus is getting broken, can give you the insights into dealing with that problem.

Develop Rage

Then, once you start understanding where these focus breaks are happening, now it's time for you to actually condition yourself to develop a rage or a hate towards focus interruptions.

You know the power of focus. You know that white, hot heat that you can produce and create amazing results in a short period of time when you're allowed to focus. You need to develop a rage towards anything that causes you to interrupt your focus.

Most of the time, it's probably going to be your own bad habits that are doing this.

Sure, there are going to be people who interrupt you and there's only so much of that you can handle, but anything you can control, now you're going to develop a rage towards it and you will simply not allow these other things, like an email message or text message to stop you.

Figure out strategies to turn the volume down or just flat out ignore it when you hear these signals coming in and stay in your mode of focus.

But until you actually have a distaste or a rage toward the interruptions, they're very seductive and you're going to be so tempted to check that text message or check that email, that they will continually break your focus unless you make a point of not letting it.

The only way you can really not let it at an effective level is when you get really, really mad at the thing.

Exercises

Let's talk about a couple of exercises that you can do today that will help you increase your focus and get you to that level of momentum you need to be at to crank out all kinds of great results.

First, practice focus. This can be anything. It could be writing for 15 minutes, totally uninterrupted, until your timer goes off.

Get some kind of audible timer that makes a sound at the end of 15 minutes, but all you're going to do for this timeframe is write. You're not going to check email, you're not even going to take your hand off the paper or you're not going to stop typing in that entire 15 minutes.

It could be something else like meditation. It could be focusing on a stopwatch for a minute at a time and not allowing your mind to wander. It can be anything, but just develop the habit of making your mind focus on a single thing or a single action.

Next, work in time blocks. If you have something that you need to get done for your business, let's say you're producing some form of work for your customer and it normally takes you 3 hours because you allow yourself to check email and voicemail while you're going through it, give yourself 30 minutes this time and see how much you can get done in that 30-minute block.

You might shock yourself. You might realize that this activity that was taking you 3 hours previously really is a 40-minute activity, when you focus on things and when you shut down your email and shut down all other distractions and leverage the momentum you get when your mind is allowed to focus on one thing.

But make focus a huge priority in your life. Take the advantage that you have, this natural instinct, this natural skill that we all have as people, that when we focus on something we get into this flow state, we get into this momentum that really, we can't be stopped.

Once we hit that, the levels of production will be amazing and your success as an entrepreneur is practically guaranteed.

8. PLAN GOALS

We're going to talk about goals and knowing your goals. Before you roll your eyes or run away screaming, don't worry. This is a short but important topic. Even if you've done the goal setting thing before and you're tired of hearing about it, I want to remind you of a few things that you may have forgotten.

This is an important topic and the best entrepreneurs are very goal-oriented and meticulously study and enhance and focus on their goals on an ongoing basis.

Let's discuss this quickly, to make sure that you're not missing anything.

I'm going to start by talking about traditional goal setting and how overrated a lot of this stuff is. If you go back to your school days, there's very likely a point in time where you learned about the smart model of goal setting, where your goals should be specific and measurable, attainable and realistic and time-based.

That's great and it has its place, but you're an online entrepreneur. You're running a business by the seat of your pants. Things are changing all the time. It's a very dynamic environment.

Even setting a "Realistic" goal is almost impossible these days, because things change so often.

Not to mention the fact that when you set goals that are very realistic, so let's take weight loss for example, it's realistic to say, "I'm going to lose 5 pounds this month." But it's not very inspiring.

If you have some weight to lose and you say, "I'm going to make it my best month ever, and I'm going to lose 25 pounds." That might be a little much, depending on your weight, but you get the idea.

If you go for something way more aggressive, something the average person would call "Unrealistic," you actually have a sense of urgency. You have a sense of inspiration. That motivational fuel doesn't exist otherwise, if you create very, very basic and conservative and "Traditional" goals.

Be Unrealistic

I want to talk about the fact that being unrealistic, when it comes to your goal setting, is actually a very good thing.

You know your goals are unrealistic when you start sharing them with other people, not entrepreneurs but regular people, and they look at you funny, like you're crazy, like you're just out to lunch and totally detached from reality.

That's actually a really good thing. If you start studying really successful entrepreneurs, they think like this all the time.

They're always pushing their own boundaries. They're setting goals that stretch them, and they're okay if they don't even hit those goals. It's more about the belief that you create in yourself when you set unrealistic goals.

That's what I want to remind you about today, is focus on what you can do to extend yourself by setting your goals in an unrealistic type of way.

Goals often get missed. You're running a business. You've probably had different plans for your week, for your month, quarter, you name it, and you set a goal of maybe some kind of revenue target or sales figure that you wanted to hit and you missed that goal and you set a new goal the next month and missed it again.

This just happens. The thing is, when we miss goals, it's not a bad thing, especially when we're operating from this mode of unrealistic, aggressive, passionate goals.

When you miss these goals that are huge, they always lead to other opportunities, and they're often really, really exciting opportunities.

I can think of times in my own business where I set a huge goal, I failed miserably but I got so far along that path that I found a new opportunity that I never would have known existed had I not set this goal.

There a people whose entire life stories have unfolded that way because they were out on the edge, doing something they really shouldn't have been doing, and it uncovered a whole new area of life for them.

Be okay with missing goals. Be okay with failing a goal, so to speak, because you know the goal is so big that even just pursuing it is going to advance you down the line. That's how you become successful as an entrepreneur.

Short-Term and Long-Term Goals

Now, let's talk a little bit of strategy here when it comes to goals: Short-term versus long-term goals.

You need to at least in your mind, have an idea of a goal that you can shoot for in the long run.

A good long-term goal can last anywhere from a 3-month to a 1-year window. It's something you're going to be working at for a longer period of time. Your short-term goals are the goals that you focus on as stepping stones to your long-term goals.

The long-term goals give you a perspective of where you want to go, and that's often changing as well, based on today's environment and today's scenarios. But that long-term goal, even as it changes, your short-term goals are what get you there.

If you have a goal to earn $1 million this year, then you can break that down to be roughly $83,000 a month. So, your short-term goal is to earn on average, $83,000 per month.

That makes it a lot easier to manage. It makes this whole idea of setting unrealistic goals come back down to earth a little bit. It makes you a little bit more rational, and other people can at least say, "Okay, he/she has a plan for this unrealistic goal."

Now, you may have been earning $5,000 a month up to now and suddenly you want to jump to $83,000. Well, that's cool. Set that goal, but also realize that there's a very good chance you're going to miss that goal.

You need to adapt your strategy, and maybe your short-term goal for the next month is, "Okay, well $83,000 was the goal last month, fell a little bit shy of that because I'd only been doing $5,000. Let's see if I can get halfway there. Let's make it $40,000 and see how close I can get."

This is the adaptive nature that goals will work for you in your business.

Share Your Goals

Another very powerful piece of goal setting is your ability to share your goals with as wide an audience as possible.

If you have a mastermind group, that's great. If you want to go onto Facebook and share some of your bigger goals with everybody in your personal world, your friends and colleagues and family, even better.

Maybe you've done this already. Maybe you've put something out there in the past and then you thought, "Oh man, now everybody knows I'm attempting to do this thing. I better get it done or I'm going to look like an idiot."

That pressure is really, really good for self-motivation, and it's also great if you just care about results more than anything else.

Be prepared to push yourself to share your goals, but then also be prepared to fail those goals, even though everybody's watching, in exchange for the lesson that you're going to learn.

If you pick an enormous goal, to earn some crazy amount of money and you declare that goal publicly and you fail in your attempt, hey, you're going to learn something along the way because I guarantee you're going to be pushing yourself way harder with everybody watching than you would if you were trying to do it silently behind the curtains, with no accountability whatsoever.

Make that your mission.

Exercises

Let's talk about some exercises.

First, write down your goals. It doesn't really matter on the length or the term of your goals. Just get in the habit of writing them down.

Maybe you want to start with writing down your goals for this week. Maybe there's a particular project you need to get finished, a certain number of calls you need to make if you're a salesperson.

Write those down and make a point of writing them down every single day.

Then, do daily tracking. Go back to look at those goals that you've set. If they're week-based goals, go back every morning and look at the actions you've taken on a daily basis that have been moving you towards them.

Review your progress, and then plan your next steps. If you take the feedback you got from the actions you took the previous day or month, then you can use that to accurately plan your next series of steps.

But the daily tracking is absolutely key, because it brings your awareness to a much more granular level, whereas if you're only checking or tracking once a month then you're going to lose control of your goals and you'll never, ever reach them.

If you do the daily tracking, you have a much greater chance at actually hitting these probably unrealistic goals you've set for yourself.

I hope this has been a great reminder for you of the type of goal setting you need to be doing as an online entrepreneur to be successful.

Make sure you get to work, and most importantly, make sure you do those exercises of writing down your goals and tracking them every single day.

9. PERSISTENCE

The foundation of any successful entrepreneur, any successful business, is rooted in persistence.
We're going to talk about cultivating persistence and how you can develop the skill and habit of persistence so that nothing can stop you and ultimately you will be able to develop a successful business.

Persistence itself is really the only difference between success and failure.

You can go back through the pages of history and look at all the entrepreneurial ventures that have succeeded and failed over time.

The people that were successful were not always successful. Every single story that you read is of somebody who went through all kinds of trials and tribulations, had one failure after another.

Ultimately, it was their persistence that led them to success. They simply refused to take no as an answer.

There is the odd case where somebody hit on their very first business venture and did really, really well right out of the gate. 99 times out of 100, the successful business is somebody who has persisted through a lot of trial and tribulation, and that's likely going to be the case for you as well.

Even if you happen to get lucky and stumble upon a business that gets out of the gate really, really quick, at some point in the growing process of yourself as an entrepreneur and your business as an organization, you will meet with challenge. It's your persistence that will carry you through.

Are you developing your persistence and are you aware of how important this skill is to your overall growth and success?

Persistence is not a short-term pain that you have to fight through to get to the other side and have an easy life. Persistence is a foundation that you have to build in to the very fiber of your being so that you live and act from a place of total commitment to your goals.

I think this is a mistake that a lot of new entrepreneurs get trapped into, and that's the idea that if I can just get through this first year or 2 years and grind it out and persist through, then things will get easier and I won't have to work as hard or struggle.

That is really clinging onto a false concept of how things really are.

No matter what level of success you reach in your business, there will always be a degree of persistence required to keep this thing going. This is true both in business and in life.

You have to realize and accept and embody the idea that persistence is something that you have to become.

If you realize it's something that is ongoing for the rest of your life, it becomes easier to start working on it and practicing it today.

As you grow and as you become a more persistent individual, later on down the road, as business gets easier, you discover new challenges or new opportunities for growth, a whole new level of persistence kicks in and it's easy for you now.

It doesn't mean there is less persistence. It doesn't mean the work gets any easier. It's all still there, but you're coming from a different mindset. You're prepared to persist through all the challenges that will inevitably pop up, because you understand they're coming and you're willing to persist.

Remember, you will always be tested, no matter how successful you become. Tests, challenges, problems, will always be there. Your persistence will always carry you through.

You might have problems, you're frustrated, your persistence is being tested and you don't even know if you want to do this anymore. That's normal, and I want to offer you a couple of ideas that you can keep at the top of your mind to remind yourself when the times get tough, which they often do as entrepreneurs, you can always try again.

I don't care what you've messed up or who you've annoyed or whatever it may be. Entrepreneurship is more about who can hold on longer than it is about anything else.

You also have to remember that as long as you're alive and kicking and still breathing, then you can try again. You can take a new approach. If you've identified a driving force, a reason why you're doing what you're doing and you know you want to achieve this thing, whatever it is in your business, then persistence isn't even a conscious effort.

It's who you are, and you've committed to this thing with all of your heart and soul and so you will just continue to do what you do until you get the result you want.

You have to know, in your heart, that your result is inevitable, even though all outside indications may be telling you otherwise, and all you have to do is hold on and keep trying new approaches and ideas and methods until you get the result.

Time is not a factor. The time is however long it takes, and your job is to continually take action and try new things and strategies and learn and grow until you get what you want.

You can do it, but do you have the persistence to get what you want?

Exercises

Let's talk about a couple of exercises that can help you strengthen your persistence.

First, I want you to make a note of times when persistence has already paid off for you in the past.

You might have to go way back. If you're not a success-based individual, if you're not good at recognizing your own successes, you may have to go way back to when you first learned to walk or something really simple where you had to try a lot of times, but you never gave up because there was no other option.

You just kept trying and you kept doing it and eventually, even though it may have taken a long time, you finally did make this thing happen.

It's probably happened many, many times even this year, maybe this month or this week. Get in touch with that side of you that has been persistent and remember all the rewards you received from being persistent.

Then you can be fully capable and comfortable with doing it more, of being persistent in all areas of life.

Next, go out and find three role models throughout history, it doesn't matter who it is, people who have demonstrated persistence that inspired you.

I guarantee, if you're an online entrepreneur, the stuff that you're persisting through right now is a fraction of what other people have had to go through in their lives. There are people who have had to endure some of the most horrific experiences, the most difficult lives, and they made it through.

Read about these people. Learn about their internal fortitude and what they had to do to get through to their end goal, and then put it back into perspective of what you're looking at right now.

I guarantee you, you'll have a new sense of energy. You'll realize it really isn't all that bad and you're going to give it another go.

This is especially important when you feel like giving up. Have those role models handy. If you need more than three, get more than three.

But just make sure you do this exercise, to remind yourself that persistence is possible and it's absolutely fundamental if you want to succeed in business.

10. PRODUCTIVITY

Now, we're going to talk about productivity, being productive. One of the most important things you can do as an online entrepreneur. Are you productive?

How would you rate your levels of productivity on a day-to-day basis?

- Do you really, really nail it every single day?

- Do you find some day your productivity is at a peak level and the next day you get nothing done?

- Do you struggle in this department?

I want to focus on this so you can put some strategies in place really, really quickly so that

you're productive all the time, not just some of the time.

It's not going to be easy, but a few quick changes can drastically increase your productivity levels, which will at the end of the day make you more money and help you become more successful in business.

First, realize productivity itself creates happiness.

Go back and think about times when you were really productive. Not just at work. It could have been at home, cleaning out the garage or doing yard work or accomplishing something.

When you were productive, at the end of that stint of production, when you looked at your work, you felt great about yourself.

This is as simple as when you play with your kids and you build a snow fort. You were productive. You put all this stuff together and at the end of it you could look at your creation and you felt good about that.

Productivity at its root gives us life, makes us feel happy, gives us inspiration.

If we can tie our happiness back to our productivity, it makes it that much easier for us to put ourselves

into situations where we will be productive on an ongoing basis.

The opposite is also true. If you're not productive, then you usually feel pretty miserable. If you have people in your life that are miserable and constantly bringing you down, take a look at their levels of productivity and I bet you won't be surprised when you see they're not as productive.

They're stuck in a rut. They're stuck in what we're talking about right now, the enemy of productivity, which is procrastination.

What is procrastination? It's delaying something you know you need to do and you're delaying it probably out of some form of fear.

It could be just fear of the pain of doing it because you really don't like writing or you don't like confronting somebody, or it could be rooted in some other fear where you're really going to be putting yourself out there. You're not getting your work done or your book done because somebody else is going to now be in a position to judge your work.

Instead of doing this thing that you should be doing that's going to make you productive and grow your life and business, you're doing something else like checking email, that you rationalize in your mind as also an equally important task, when it's nowhere near as important as this productive task you should be doing right now.

Our bodies are naturally built this way. We feel horrible when we're not productive.

Procrastination makes us feel horrible. The only antidote is to turn it around and become productive, and that's the key.

Real productivity comes from the necessity to deliver.

If you are on the hook, if you have a deadline and there's no way out, you get a lot more productive than if there's a soft deadline or a floating deadline or no deadline at all.

Think about anytime you've set a project for yourself. If there was a deadline and there were people waiting on you, you got it done. If there was nobody waiting, you didn't get it done. Maybe you did, but you're an extraordinary individual. Chances are, you did not get it done.

Knowing this, you can start scheduling your days and your agendas so that you put yourself in a position on purpose, where you have to deliver because there are people waiting, there are agendas or deadlines to be hit and if you don't there are consequences to pay.

That's not always easy to make that decision, but it's the only way to guarantee productivity on a day-to-day basis.

You might motivate yourself. You might watch a bunch of motivational videos or listen to really energetic music and get pumped up and increase your productivity in the short term.

But without that natural, built-in necessity to deliver, I guarantee your productivity will dip unless you've absolutely conditioned yourself to do this on a daily basis.

Most of us haven't, so we have to create these instances or these forums that lock us in to delivering on our commitments. That's where productivity comes in.

Exercises

Let's talk about some exercises that will help you become more productive. There are two things you need to do.

First, make a list of when your productivity peaked. Why did it peak? Think back. It's probably because you were locked in. You had some kind of agenda to deliver on, somebody was expecting something of you and you got it done.

Then, go back and make another list of when your productivity dipped. Why did it dip? Look at the things that cause you to procrastinate, cause you to become less productive.

How did you feel when you were less productive? Remind yourself of that awful feeling of not getting things done.

Then, go ahead and lock yourself into more and more situations where you will be forced to be productive. Make it a daily habit.

Maybe your new habit is every single day you commit to someone or to a group of people that you will deliver something. Just by doing this, you will be a more productive individual.

This will help you make productivity a normal part your daily life. Now you're making the productivity more important than the procrastination, more important than the fears and you will get results.

To Your Success!

ABOUT THE AUTHOR

Edward Spade is an entrepreneur with decades of executive leadership and corporate consulting experience. He has a passion to help others succeed and is actively pursuing this through information marketing and providing others with tools and techniques to get their message and products out to the world.

He has consulted and worked with numerous companies in both the private and public sectors by providing corporate communications, social media management, social media branding, and corporate image consulting along with media and public relations at local, national, and international levels.

Edward was co-founder of a media-relations firm in central Florida, which under his leadership grew to become one of Florida's largest privately held firms which specialized in publicly traded companies. After successfully launching many private companies to publicly traded status he decided to spend more time with his family and discovered a way to utilize his experience and expertise in assisting his wife to achieve her goal of establishing a name brand in the wedding industry.

Edward has held both a Real Estate license and a Mortgage Broker license. He has a wonderful wife, Cassie, and currently has three great children: Eddie, Olivia, and Timothy.

"THINK RIGHT, DO RIGHT, & BE RIGHT...

DO IT NOW!"

www.ingramcontent.com/pod-product-compliance
Lightning Source LLC
Chambersburg PA
CBHW052333220526
45472CB00001B/395